LES PETITS PLATS
FRANÇAIS
SIMON & SCHUSTER
ILLUSTRATED

meringue magic

ALISA MOROV

Photography by Deirdre Rooney
Styling by Élodie Rambaud

SIMON &
SCHUSTER
ILLUSTRATED

London · New York · Sydney · Toronto
A CBS COMPANY

English language edition published in Great Britain by
Simon & Schuster UK Ltd, 2011
A CBS Company

Copyright © Marabout 2009

SIMON AND SCHUSTER
ILLUSTRATED BOOKS
Simon & Schuster UK
222 Gray's Inn Road
London WC1X 8HB
www.simonandschuster.co.uk

This book is copyright under the Berne Convention.
No reproduction without permission.
All rights reserved.

The right of Alisa Morov to be identified as the Author of this Work has been
asserted by her in accordance with sections 77 and 78 of the Copyright,
Designs and Patents Act, 1988.

1 2 3 4 5 6 7 8 9 10

Translation: Prudence Ivey
Copy editor English language: Nicki Lampon

Colour reproduction by Dot Gradations Ltd, UK
Printed and bound in U.A.E.

ISBN 978-0-85720-250-5

Contents

Introduction

On my first visit to France, I saw bakery windows with stacks of beautiful, cloud-like confections and discovered that these were meringues. They were lovely to look at, and completely different to any American meringue. So I tried one. It was sad and disappointing. That day, that particular specimen was very dry, crumbly, too sweet and not worth eating. So I gave up on meringues.

Many years later, I had a meringue epiphany. My friend and colleague, Deirdre, proclaimed her love of a fresh-baked meringue with plain, unsweetened, whipped cream. I expressed serious doubt. But I trusted her, and she started to show me how to make a basic meringue with thick whipped cream. Fresh (no more than 5 days old), baked to perfection, the light crunchy exterior protected a chewy delicious interior. The whipped cream was the perfect contrast and accompaniment. And it was good.

Fireworks started going off in my head. Perhaps this magical combination of egg whites and sugar could be altered… made into other shapes… made savoury… made to float. I became inspired, obsessed (there's a fine line between the two). My research on how and why a meringue works led to many experiments and

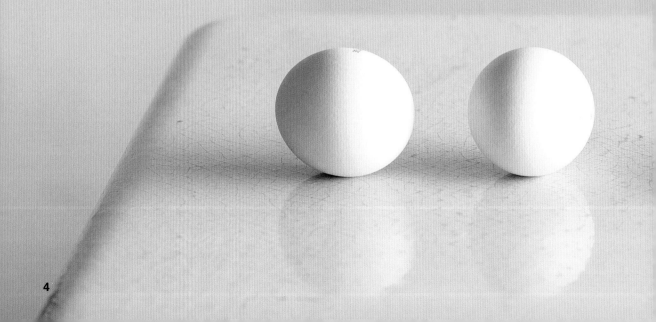

inventions. With everything I decided to cook or eat I thought: 'How could a meringue be put into this dish?' I was making notes, brainstorming wherever I went. I fell in love with the classics, using them as a foundation for other sweet meringues. But I didn't find anyone else making savoury meringues in the way I was now thinking and working.

Taste is always my first objective. Combining wonderful, surprising flavours and textures in an entirely new way has brought me so much joy. I hope that you have just as much fun with my sweet and savoury meringues as I do.

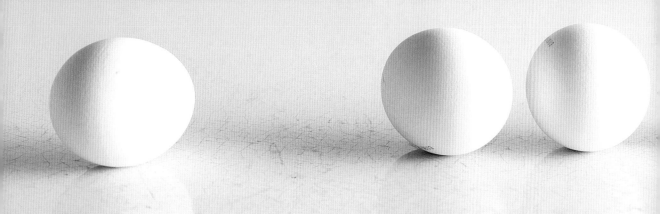

Equipment

Electric mixer with whisk attachment

Spatula, spoons and whisks

Measuring cups and spoons

Scales

Baking parchment

Baking sheets or trays

Cooling rack

Piping bags with nozzles of different shapes and sizes

Start with simple, everyday ingredients and equipment. You'll end up with magic!

All about egg whites...

Beating egg whites

When you whisk an egg white, you force air into it. Sugar adds stiffness. The standard 50 g (1¾ oz) of sugar to 1 egg white holds for most of the sweet meringues in this book. I discovered that to make a more savoury meringue, you can reduce the ratio to 30–40 g (1–1½ oz), depending on the other ingredients. It is essential to follow the recipe and add ingredients in the right order.

Fat – the beaten egg white's enemy

If beaten into egg whites, fats cause a meringue to collapse. This is the desired effect in the Chocolate coriander cookies with macadamia nuts (page 24), but it is not what you want when swirling chocolate or fruit into an unbaked meringue. You should gently fold these ingredients into the beaten egg whites by hand.

Moisture – another enemy

Before starting, preheat the oven for 20 minutes and prepare a baking sheet with baking parchment. I don't like using silicone baking sheets for meringues. They allow moisture to form and get trapped and then you get a bad meringue.

Bowls and eggs

To whisk your egg whites, choose stainless steel bowls or, even better, copper. They must be perfectly clean and dry. Use medium-sized eggs that are at least 3 days old – they should not be too fresh.

No yolk in the whites!

Be very careful when you separate the egg yolks from the whites: the slightest drop of yolk, which contains fat, will completely destroy the meringue. Use the empty egg shell or a clean, metal spoon to remove any yolk. Do not use your fingers – the natural oils from your skin will also ruin the meringue.

Timing is everything

Before beating the egg whites, keep them at room temperature for 30 minutes. Once the eggs have been whisked, continue with the recipe at once. The whisked eggs will melt like snow in the sun if left to sit for more than 2 minutes.

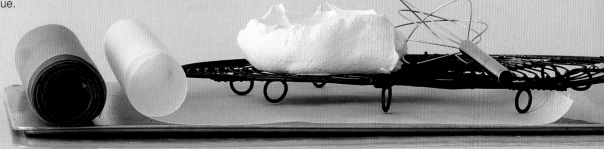

Finally, making meringues

From egg whites to meringue

Whisk the egg whites on a medium speed for a minute, then increase to a high speed. The longer the whisking time, the more volume you will get and the more stable the meringue. Add sugar only after the whites have formed soft peaks. Add the sugar gradually, a few spoonfuls at a time, and whisk until the sugar is dissolved. Touch the foam with your finger – if it feels gritty, keep going. The mixture is ready for baking when it doesn't slide off a spoon and holds its shape.

Cooking

Oven temperature is essential for a happy meringue. Having an independent thermometer in your oven will ensure that the temperature is right. If your oven or baking sheets are only large enough to bake half the recipe for small cookies, dippers and crackers, have two pieces of baking parchment ready. Pipe out the remaining meringue on to the second piece of parchment, ready to go into the oven as soon as the first is done.

Storage

Once cooked, it's important to leave your meringues to cool completely.

Baked, cooled meringues can be kept in very airtight containers and still be wonderful for up to 5 days, depending on their ingredients.

Shaping meringues

Spoons and spatulas

Spoons and spatulas of all sizes are the perfect tools for making meringues of different shapes – large or small billowy clouds, thin wafers like those in the Meringue and caviar millefeuille (page 64), free-form baskets to be filled with something savoury or sweet...

Piping bags

With a little practice, piping bags and nozzles are easy to use and really fun. However, avoid tiny nozzles used for detailed decoration. Use larger nozzles for meringues, even when making a fine meringue. The stiffer the meringue mixture before it is piped, the better the meringue will keep its shape. With simple, fluted nozzles, you will always get beautiful results.

Opposite:

1. Small, round nozzle

2. Large, star-shaped nozzle

3. Zigzag nozzle

4. Large, round nozzle

5. Leaf-shaped nozzle

6. Medium, star-shaped nozzle

7. Ribbon nozzle

8. Medium, round nozzle

1

2

3

4

5

6

7

8

Classic meringues

Preparation time: 10 minutes
Cooking time: 1½–2 hours
Makes 6 large meringues

2 egg whites, at room temperature
100 g (3½ oz) caster sugar

Preheat the oven to 90°C (fan oven 70°C), Gas Mark ¼.

Line a baking sheet with baking parchment.

Place the egg whites in a large metal bowl. Using an electric whisk, whisk on a medium speed for about 1 minute. The egg whites will turn to foam and grow in volume. Increase to a high speed and continue whisking until soft peaks begin to form.

Still whisking, add the sugar gradually, a few spoonfuls at a time, whisking for 20–30 seconds between each addition. Continue to whisk until the whites are eight times their original volume, the sugar has dissolved and the mixture is stiff and shiny. Touch the foam with your finger – if it feels gritty, keep whisking. The mixture is ready for baking when it doesn't slide off a spoon and it holds its shape.

Spoon the mixture on to the parchment-lined baking sheet in beautiful cloud shapes, or put the entire mixture into a piping bag and pipe shapes on to the baking sheet. This recipe will make six 10 cm (4 inch) round, cloud-shaped meringues.

Place the meringues in the preheated oven for about 1½–2 hours or until they are dry to the touch and still white in colour. Allow to cool completely before removing from the baking parchment. These can be stored in a very airtight container for up to 5 days.

Note: The recipes for smaller, piped meringues, require a shorter baking time.

American meringues & Italian meringues

American meringues

Preparation time: 10 minutes
Cooking time: 20–30 minutes
Makes 4 large meringues

2 egg whites, at room temperature
50 g (1¾ oz) caster sugar
1 teaspoon cream of tartar
1 teaspoon cornflour
½ teaspoon vanilla extract

Preheat the oven to 170°C (fan oven 150°C), Gas Mark 3. Line a baking sheet with baking parchment.

Whisk the egg whites until soft peaks begin to form. Still whisking, gradually add the sugar, a few spoonfuls at a time, whisking for 30 seconds between each addition. Add the cream of tartar and cornflour and whisk until firm peaks form. Continue to whisk until the egg whites are eight times their original volume and the mixture is stiff and shiny. Add the vanilla extract and whisk for another 30 seconds. The mixture is ready for baking when it doesn't slide off a spoon and it holds its shape.

Spoon the mixture on to the baking sheet in pretty cloud shapes or use a piping bag.

Place the meringues in the preheated oven for around 20–30 minutes until they are dry to the touch but still white in colour. Leave to cool completely before removing from the baking parchment. They will keep for 2 days in an airtight container.

Italian meringues

Preparation time: 10 minutes
Cooking time: 20–30 minutes
Makes 6 large meringues

4 egg whites, at room temperature
200 g (7 oz) caster sugar
½ teaspoon vanilla extract

Preheat the oven to 170°C (fan oven 150°C), Gas Mark 3.

Line a large baking sheet with baking parchment.

Place the egg whites and sugar in a metal bowl and place over a pan of gently simmering water. Whisk with a hand whisk for about 2–4 minutes while the mixture cooks. Touch the foam with your finger – if it feels gritty, keep whisking. Remove the bowl from the heat.

Using an electric whisk, whisk slowly for 10 seconds, gradually increasing the speed to high. Continue whisking until the meringue is cool to the touch and stiff shiny peaks form. This will take about 8 minutes. Mix in the vanilla extract and whisk for another minute.

Spoon the mixture on to the baking sheet in pretty cloud shapes or use a piping bag.

Place the meringues in the preheated oven for around 20–30 minutes until they are dry to the touch but still white in colour. Leave to cool completely before removing from the baking parchment.

Brown sugar meringues & Coffee meringues

Brown sugar meringues

Preparation time: 15 minutes
Cooking time: 15–25 minutes
Makes 6 large meringues

2 egg whites, at room temperature
55 g (2 oz) light brown sugar
a pinch of cream of tartar
a pinch of salt
½ teaspoon vanilla extract

Preheat the oven to 150°C (fan oven 130°C), Gas Mark 2. Line a baking sheet with baking parchment.

Following the Classic meringues recipe (page 12), whisk the egg whites until they form stiff peaks. Add the brown sugar and cream of tartar bit by bit, whisking until the mixture is stiff and shiny. Add the salt and vanilla extract and whisk for another 30 seconds. The mixture is ready for baking when it doesn't slide off a spoon and it holds its shape.

Spoon the meringue on to the baking sheet in beautiful cloud shapes, or put the entire mixture in a piping bag and pipe your desired shapes on to the baking sheet.

Place the meringues in the preheated oven for 15–25 minutes or until they are dry to the touch. Because of the light brown sugar, they will have a caramel colour. Allow to cool completely before removing from the baking parchment. Store in an airtight container for up to 3 days.

Coffee meringues

Preparation time: 20 minutes
Cooking time: 1½ hours
Makes 6 large meringues

1 teaspoon instant coffee
1 teaspoon coffee extract
2 egg whites, at room temperature
100 g (3½ oz) caster sugar

Preheat the oven to 90°C (fan oven 70°C), Gas Mark ¼. Line a baking sheet with baking parchment.

In a small bowl, combine the instant coffee with the coffee extract until smooth. Set aside.

Following the Classic meringues recipe (page 12), whisk the egg whites to stiff peaks then gradually whisk in the sugar until you have a stiff and shiny mixture. Add the coffee and whisk for 30 seconds or until fully blended. The mixture is ready for baking when it doesn't slide off a spoon and it holds its shape.

Spoon the mixture on to the baking sheet in beautiful cloud shapes, or put the entire mixture in a piping bag and pipe your desired shapes on to the baking sheet.

Place the meringues in the preheated oven for about 1½ hours, or until they are dry to the touch but have not changed colour. Allow to cool completely before removing from the baking parchment. They can be stored in an airtight container for up to 5 days.

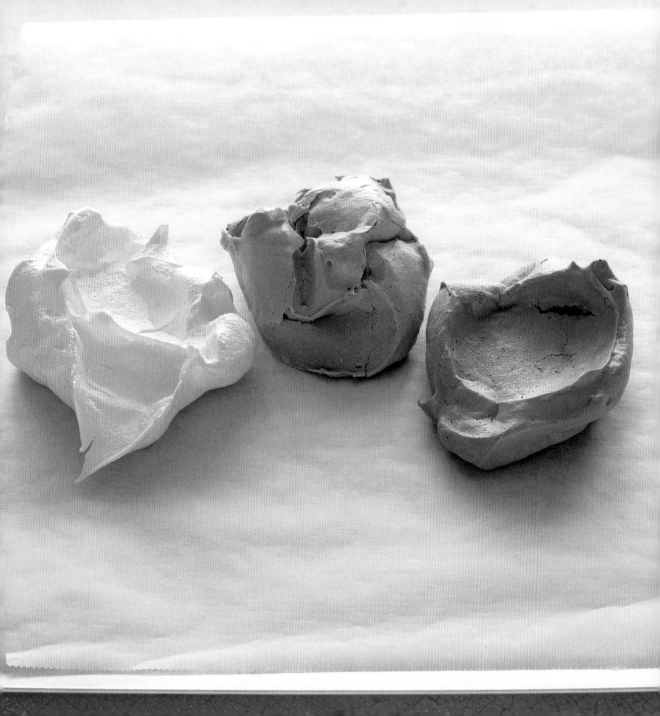

Meringue cream sandwich (Deirdre's favourite)

This is what caused my meringue epiphany. Something simple in its parts but sublime in its whole. Eat slowly and savour the experience.

Preparation time: 30 minutes
Cooking time: 1 hour
Makes 6 meringue sandwiches

Meringues
2 egg whites, at room temperature
100 g (3½ oz) caster sugar

Whipped cream
330 ml (11½ fl oz) double cream
250 g (8¾ oz) mascarpone
¼ teaspoon vanilla extract

Following the recipe on page 12, make up the Classic meringues mixture.

Form the mixture into 12 x 6 cm (2½ inch) rounds. Bake for 1 hour, or until the meringues are dry to the touch and still white in colour. Allow to cool completely before removing from the baking parchment.

For the cream, whisk on high for 5–8 minutes until thick and peaks have formed. Add the mascarpone and whisk for 1–2 minutes. Add the vanilla extract and whisk until fully combined. The cream can be made and stored in the refrigerator for up to 2 hours.

Just before serving, sandwich two meringues together with 2 tablespoons of whipped cream.

Variations: You could also use Brown sugar meringues (page 16) or Coffee meringues (page 16).

Liquorice meringues, Oreo style

This tastes like an Oreo cookie. The blend of liquorice powder, egg whites and black food colouring surprised me with this gorgeous purple colour.

Preparation time: 30 minutes
Cooking time: 20 minutes
Makes 6–7 meringue sandwiches

Liquorice meringues
2 egg whites, at room temperature
100 g (3½ oz) caster sugar
½ teaspoon liquorice powder
a pinch of salt
¼ teaspoon black food colouring

Whipped cream
330 ml (11½ fl oz) double cream
250 g (8¾ oz) mascarpone
¼ teaspoon vanilla extract

Preheat the oven to 90°C (fan oven 70°C), Gas Mark ¼.

Line a baking sheet with baking parchment. Prepare a piping bag with a five-point star nozzle.

Place the egg whites in a large metal bowl. Using an electric whisk, begin whisking on a medium speed as if you are making Classic meringues (page 12). Gradually add the sugar and continue to whisk until the egg whites are eight times their original volume, the sugar has dissolved and the mixture is stiff and shiny. Slowly add the liquorice powder, salt and food colouring. The mixture is ready for baking when it doesn't slide off a spoon and it holds its shape.

Put the mixture into the piping bag. Pipe 6 cm (2½ inch) rings on to the baking sheet. (This recipe will make 12–14 rings.) Bake for about 20 minutes or until they are dry to the touch and just starting to brown on the edges. Allow to cool completely before removing from the baking parchment. Store in a very airtight container for up to 5 days.

Whisk the cream on high for 5–8 minutes until thick and peaks form. Add the mascarpone and whisk for 1–2 minutes. Add the vanilla extract and whisk again.

Just before serving, sandwich two meringues together with 1–2 tablespoons of cream.

Tip: If your oven or baking sheets are not large enough to bake all the meringues, have two pieces of baking parchment ready. Pipe out the remaining meringue on to the second piece of paper, ready to go in the oven as soon as the first is done.

Vanilla and passion fruit meringues with crème anglaise

Vanilla and cream go so well with passion fruit. Okay…so is there anything that vanilla and cream don't go well with? The crème anglaise can be made a few days in advance, and provides a solution as to what to do with the egg yolks! With passion fruit in them, these meringues do not keep more than 2 days.

Preparation time: 20 minutes
Cooking time: 1½ hours
Makes 6 meringues

Vanilla and passion fruit meringues
1 vanilla pod
4 egg whites, at room temperature
100 g (3½ oz) caster sugar
4 tablespoons passion fruit seeds (approx. 2 medium fruits)

Crème anglaise
250 ml (8¾ fl oz) double cream
4 egg yolks
3 tablespoons caster sugar
1 teaspoon vanilla extract

Preheat the oven to 90°C (fan oven 70°C), Gas Mark ¼. Line a baking sheet with baking parchment.

Split the vanilla pod lengthwise and scrape out all the seeds. Set the seeds aside.

Follow the Classic meringues recipe (page 12) by whisking the egg whites and sugar until the egg whites are eight times their original volume, the sugar has dissolved and the mixture is stiff and shiny.

Add the vanilla seeds and whisk for another 30 seconds. Add the passion fruit seeds in a swirling pattern. Using a rubber spatula, gently fold in three or four times. Do not mix well.

Spoon the mixture on to the baking sheet in big beautiful shapes. Place in the oven for about 1½ hours, or until they are dry to the touch and still white in colour. Allow to cool completely before removing from the baking parchment.

For the crème anglaise, place the cream in a heavy-based saucepan. Bring to a soft rolling boil then remove from the heat. Using an electric mixer and a paddle attachment, beat the egg yolks and sugar together until very thick and pale yellow. Slowly add the heated cream, beat well on a medium speed, add the vanilla extract and mix again for 20 seconds.

Pour the custard back into the saucepan and cook on a very low heat, stirring continually until it thickens and coats the back of a spoon (about 10 minutes). Remove from the heat, strain through a sieve into a clean bowl and refrigerate immediately with cling film across the top. This prevents a skin from forming.

When cooled, serve with the meringues for dipping or drizzling on top.

Tip: The crème anglaise will keep for 4–5 days in the fridge.

Chocolate coriander cookies with macadamia nuts

I really love the combination of coriander and chocolate. These slightly crunchy, nicely chewy cookies, washed down with a glass of cold milk, are a pure delight.

Preparation time: 15 minutes
Cooking time: 35 minutes
Makes around 12 cookies

65 g (2¼ oz) macadamia nuts
4 egg whites, at room temperature
200 g (7 oz) caster sugar
a pinch of salt
2 teaspoons ground coriander
25 g (1 oz) cocoa powder

Preheat the oven to 125°C (fan oven 105°C), Gas Mark ½. Line a baking sheet with baking parchment.

Chop the nuts into halves or thirds. Place on the baking sheet and toast in the oven until they start to develop a light golden colour. Remove from the baking sheet and set aside. You can use the same baking sheet and paper for baking the cookies.

Place the egg whites in a large metal bowl. Using an electric whisk, whisk on a medium speed for about 1 minute. The whites will turn to foam and begin to increase in volume. Increase the speed to high and continue until soft peaks begin to form. Still whisking, add the sugar a few spoonfuls at a time, whisking for 20–30 seconds after each addition. Continue to whisk until the egg whites are eight times their original volume, the sugar has dissolved and the mixture is stiff and shiny.

Add the salt and coriander and whisk for 20 seconds. Slowly add the cocoa powder. The volume of the meringue will decrease when you add the cocoa powder but don't worry.

Spoon the meringue mixture on to the baking sheet, making 12 x 6–7 cm (2½–2¾ inch) circles. Drop 4–5 pieces of macadamia nut on to each circle.

Bake for 35 minutes. Allow the cookies to cool completely before removing from the baking parchment. Store in an airtight container for up to 4 days.

Variation: You could use ground cardamom in place of the coriander.

Coconut and sweet curry cookies

A few years ago I saw a newspaper article entitled 'Cookies, Coconut, Curry and Nutmeg'. I got so excited about the idea of cookies with these three ingredients. Well… the article was actually a list of Indian recipes with some simple butter cookies. However, thoughts of cookies with these three ingredients stuck with me. It was too good an idea to ignore.

Preparation time: 10 minutes
Cooking time: 20 minutes
Makes 20–24 cookies

60 g (2 oz) desiccated coconut
2 egg whites, at room temperature
100 g (3½ oz) caster sugar
½ teaspoon curry powder
1 teaspoon grated nutmeg
¼ teaspoo vanilla extract
grated zest of 1 lime
100 ml (3½ fl oz) coconut milk

Preheat the oven to 90°C (fan oven 70°C), Gas Mark ¼. Line a baking sheet with baking parchment. Sprinkle 20 g (¾ oz) of desiccated coconut on to the parchment. Prepare a piping bag with a 7–8 mm (⅓ inch) ribbon nozzle.

Place the egg whites in a large metal bowl. Using an electric whisk, whisk on a medium speed for about 1 minute. The whites will turn to foam and begin to increase in volume. Increase the speed to high and continue until soft peaks begin to form. Still whisking, add the sugar a few spoonfuls at a time, whisking for 20–30 seconds after each addition. Continue to whisk until the egg whites are eight times their original volume, the sugar has dissolved and the mixture is stiff and shiny.

Slowly add the curry powder, nutmeg and vanilla extract and whisk for 20–30 seconds. Add 20 g (¾ oz) of desiccated coconut and whisk for another 15 seconds.

Put the mixture into the piping bag. For each cookie, pipe ribbons, touching each other and going back and forth, forming a 5 cm (2 inch) rectangle. Space the meringues about 4 cm (1½ inches) apart. Sprinkle over the remaining coconut and the lime zest.

Bake for about 20 minutes or until the cookies are dry to the touch and just starting to turn golden. Allow to cool completely before removing from the baking parchment. They can be stored in a very airtight container for up to 5 days.

Serve with the coconut milk for dipping.

Tip: If your oven or baking sheets are not large enough to bake all the cookies, have two pieces of baking parchment ready. Pipe out the remaining meringue on to the second piece of paper, ready to go in the oven as soon as the first is done.

Peanut butter and jelly meringue sandwich

PB & J – peanut butter and jelly – is the sandwich that kids across America grow up with. But this is no basic sandwich. Using meringue shaped like sandwich bread, and making a buttercream filling with peanut butter, I have turned PB & J into a sophisticated dessert.

Preparation time: 30 minutes
Cooking time: 30–45 minutes
Makes 3 sandwiches (serves 6)

Meringues
2 egg whites, at room temperature
100 g (3½ oz) caster sugar

Filling
250 g (8¾ oz) peanut butter, at room temperature
200 g (7 oz) salted butter, at room temperature
225 g (8 oz) icing sugar
3 tablespoons strawberry jam

Preheat the oven to 90°C (fan oven 70°C), Gas Mark ¼. Line a baking sheet with baking parchment

Make the meringue mixture by following the recipe for Classic meringues (page 12). With a knife or spatula, form six 10 cm (4 inch) square, 1–1.5 cm (½–¾ inch) thick meringue 'breads' on the baking parchment. Since the 'breads' are thinner than regular meringues, only bake for 30–45 minutes. Allow to cool completely before removing gently from the baking parchment. The meringues will keep for 5 days in an airtight container.

For the buttercream, using an electric mixer, mix the peanut butter and salted butter until well combined. Slowly add the sugar and mix well. The buttercream can be used immediately or stored in the refrigerator for 5 days. Bring to room temperature before assembling the sandwiches.

With a knife or spatula, gently spread a 1 cm (½ inch) layer of buttercream on to one meringue 'bread' slice. Gently spread 1 tablespoon of strawberry jam on top of the cream. Place another meringue slice on top and slice diagonally with a very sharp knife. It is probably easiest to eat this sandwich with a knife and fork.

Pistachio and cardamom langue de chat

Mint tea, the Casbah, stories of *1001 Nights*… these little meringues will transport you to exotic places.

Preparation time: 15 minutes
Cooking time: 20 minutes
Makes 20 meringues

50 g (1¾ oz) pistachio nuts
2 egg whites, at room temperature
100 g (3½ oz) caster sugar
½ teaspoon ground cardamom
1 drop green food colouring
1–2 drops pistachio extract
1 tablespoon silver balls, for
   decoration

Preheat the oven to 90°C (fan oven 70°C), Gas Mark ¼. Line a baking sheet with baking parchment. Prepare a piping bag with a medium-sized round nozzle.

Toast the pistachio nuts in the oven for 10 minutes. Allow to cool for 10 minutes, then roughly chop. Set aside.

Place the egg whites in a large metal bowl. Using an electric whisk, whisk on a medium speed for about 1 minute. The whites will turn to foam and begin to increase in volume. Increase the speed to high and continue until soft peaks begin to form. Still whisking, add the sugar a few spoonfuls at a time, whisking for 20–30 seconds after each addition. Continue to whisk until the egg whites are eight times their original volume, the sugar has dissolved and the mixture is stiff and shiny. Slowly add the cardamom, food colouring and pistachio extract, whisking until the mixture is a uniform colour. It is ready for baking when it doesn't slide off a spoon and it holds its shape.

Put the mixture into the piping bag. For each langue de chat, pipe a line about 6 cm (2½ inches) long, then pipe back up along the side, pulling the bag to make a little peak. Space the meringues about 3 cm (1¼ inches) apart. Sprinkle over the chopped pistachios and silver balls.

Bake for about 20 minutes or until the meringues are dry to the touch and just starting to turn a little golden on the peaks. Allow to cool completely before removing from the baking parchment. The meringues can be stored in an airtight container for up to 5 days.

Tip: If your oven or baking sheets are not large enough to bake all the meringues, have two pieces of baking parchment ready. Pipe out the remaining meringue on to the second piece of paper, ready to go in the oven as soon as the first is done.

Little pink meringues with pink Champagne jellies

My meringue obsession has left nothing untouched! I do believe, however, that these will please the Champagne gods. Be sure to make them well in advance – the Champagne jelly will take at least 8 hours to set in the fridge.

Preparation time: 15 minutes + 8 hours chilling
Cooking time: 20 minutes
Makes 14 meringues

Pink Champagne jellies
50 ml (1¾ fl oz) sugar cane syrup
3 sheets of gelatine
375 ml (13¼ fl oz) pink Champagne

Meringues
2 egg whites, at room temperature
100 g (3½ oz) caster sugar
½ teaspoon powdered red food colouring or 1 drop liquid red food colouring (see Tip)

For the Champagne jelly, place the sugar syrup in a large saucepan. Warm on a low heat while you soak the gelatine according to the packet instructions. Squeeze out the excess water and add the gelatine to the sugar syrup. Stir continuously until the gelatine is dissolved. Remove from the heat and add the Champagne, stirring until well combined. Pour the mixture into a shallow-sided tray and chill for at least 8 hours, until it has set. You can keep the jelly in the refrigerator for up to 5 days.

Preheat the oven to 90°C (fan oven 70°C), Gas Mark ¼. Line a baking sheet with baking parchment. Prepare a piping bag with a 4 cm (1½ inch) star nozzle.

Following the recipe for Classic meringues (page 12), whisk the egg whites and gradually add the sugar until the mixture is stiff and shiny. Add the food colouring and whisk well until the colour is even.

Put the meringue mixture into the piping bag. Pipe 3.5 cm (1¼ inch) circles on the baking parchment, working the spirals inward and pulling up to a point in the middle. Make 28 meringues, spaced about 3 cm (1¼ inches) apart. Bake for about 20 minutes or until they are dry to the touch. Allow to cool completely before removing from the baking parchment. The meringues can be stored in an airtight container for up to 5 days.

Assemble the meringues just before serving. Cut out circular jellies using a 3.5 cm (1¼ inch) round cookie cutter. Remove from the tray with a flat spatula or knife and place one Champagne jelly between two pink meringues. They will stick to each other after about a minute.

Tip: If you are unable to find powdered food colouring, you can use liquid, but only use 1 drop. The liquid will change the consistency of the meringue.

Meringue biscuits with four sauces

Preparation time: 10 minutes +
preparation times for the sauces
Cooking time: 15–20 minutes
Serves 6

Meringues
2 egg whites, at room temperature
100 g (3½ oz) caster sugar

Chocolate sauce
150 g (5¼ oz) dark or milk chocolate

Nectarine sauce
2 nectarines, peeled, stoned and
cut into small pieces
120 ml (4¼ fl oz) water
100 g (3½ oz) caster sugar

Salted caramel sauce (Recipe
borrowed from *De Caramel Plein
La Bouche* by Trish Deseine)
100 g (3½ oz) caster sugar
2 tablespoons water
50 g (1¾ oz) salted butter
1 rounded tablespoon mascarpone

Crème anglaise
250 ml (8¾ fl oz) double cream
4 egg yolks, at room temperature
100 g (3½ oz) caster sugar
1 teaspoon vanilla extract

Preheat the oven to 90°C (fan oven 70°C), Gas Mark ¼. Line a baking sheet with baking parchment. Prepare a piping bag with a flat serrated nozzle.

Follow the Classic meringues recipe (page 12) to make the meringues. Place the mixture into the piping bag. Form 8–10 cm (3¼–4 inch) long meringues by piping with a rippled motion, pulling up to a point at the end. Space the meringues about 3 cm (1¼ inches) apart. Bake for about 15–20 minutes or until they are dry to the touch and still white. Allow to cool completely before removing from the baking parchment. The meringues can be stored in an airtight container for up to 5 days.

For the chocolate sauce, melt the chocolate over a pan of simmering water or in the microwave. Be careful not to overheat the chocolate if using the microwave.

For the nectarine sauce, put the nectarines, water and sugar in a medium-sized saucepan. Bring to the boil, reduce the heat to low and simmer for 15 minutes, stirring often. Place in a bowl, cool and refrigerate before using.

For the caramel sauce, melt the sugar in the water to get a caramel. Away from the heat, add the butter. The caramel will harden in places but this does not matter. Add the mascarpone and mix well. Return to the heat to dissolve the remaining sugar crystals. Serve warm or leave to cool. The sauce will keep for 4–5 days in the fridge.

For the crème anglaise, follow the method on page 22.

Maple syrup meringues with blueberries

In addition to furthering the consumption of meringues, I am thinking of starting a campaign to use maple syrup much more often.

Preparation time: 10 minutes
Cooking time: 40–60 minutes
Makes 8–10 meringues

Maple syrup meringues
2 egg whites, at room temperature
40 g (1½ oz) caster sugar
¼ teaspoon cream of tartar
120 ml (4¼ fl oz) maple syrup

To serve
250 g (8¾ oz) blueberries
3–4 tablespoons maple syrup

Preheat the oven to 90°C (fan oven 70°C), Gas Mark ¼.

Line a baking sheet with baking parchment. Prepare a piping bag with a medium-sized round nozzle.

Place the egg whites in a large metal bowl. Using an electric whisk, whisk on a medium speed for about 1 minute. The whites will turn to foam and begin to increase in volume. Increase the speed to high and continue until soft peaks begin to form. Still whisking, add the sugar a few spoonfuls at a time, whisking for 20–30 seconds after each addition.

Add the cream of tartar and continue to whisk until the egg whites are six times their original volume, the sugar has dissolved and the mixture is stiff and shiny. Add the maple syrup and whisk for another 30 seconds.

Put the meringue mixture into the piping bag. Pipe 7 cm (2¾ inch) circles on the baking sheet, working the spiral inward and pulling up to a point in the middle. Space the meringues about 3 cm (1¼ inches) apart.

Bake for about 40–60 minutes or until the meringues are dry to the touch and the tip is just beginning to be slightly darker than the rest. Allow to cool completely before removing from the baking parchment. The meringues can be stored in an airtight container for up to 3 days.

Serve by placing two meringues on a plate with a handful of blueberries. Drizzle a little maple syrup over both and serve with coffee, milk or whipped cream.

Meringue wafers with Sauternes jellies

This light dessert leaves you feeling just a little bit tipsy. It's not for the young… but definitely for the young at heart.

Preparation time: 25 minutes +
  8 hours chilling
Cooking time: 20 minutes
Serves 6

Sauternes jelly
400 ml (14 fl oz) Sauternes
4 sheets of gelatine

Meringues
2 egg whites, at room temperature
100 g (3½ oz) caster sugar

Place the Sauternes in a saucepan and warm over a low heat while you soak the gelatine according to the packet instructions. Squeeze out the excess water and add the gelatine to the Sauternes. Stir continuously until it is dissolved. Remove from the heat and divide between six 4–5 cm (1½–2 inch) round moulds. Refrigerate for at least 8 hours, until the jellies have set. You can keep them for up to 5 days in the refrigerator.

Preheat the oven to 90°C (fan oven 70°C), Gas Mark ¼. Line a baking sheet with baking parchment.

Make the meringue mixture by following the recipe for Classic meringues (page 12).

Using a spatula or a pastry brush, paint 1–2 cm (½–¾ inch) thick and 12–16 cm (4½–6¼ inch) long strokes of meringue on to the baking sheet. Bake for about 20 minutes or until they are dry to the touch and still white in colour. Allow to cool completely before removing from the baking parchment. This will make more than you need, but they store in an airtight container for up to 5 days.

To remove the jellies from the moulds, place in a shallow bowl of hot water for 10 seconds, then turn upside down on to serving plates and lift the moulds. Serve with the meringue wafers.

Lemon meringue pie

This is the real deal! The lemon filling is topped with American or soft meringue. Whenever my mother made this pie, it was as if magic was being performed in our kitchen.

Preparation time: 30 minutes +
2 hours resting for the pastry +
cooling
Cooking time: 30–45 minutes
Serves 8

Pastry
70 g (2½ oz) unsalted butter, at
room temperature
60 g (2 oz) icing sugar
2 large egg yolks
220 g (7¾ oz) plain flour
¼ teaspoon salt
2 teaspoons double cream

Lemon filling
3 egg yolks
4 large eggs
225 g (8 oz) caster sugar
175 ml (6¼ fl oz) lemon juice
grated zest of 1 lemon
120 g (4¼ oz) butter, softened

American meringue topping
3 egg whites, at room temperature
1 teaspoon cream of tartar
1 teaspoon cornflour
50 g (1¾ oz) caster sugar
½ teaspoon vanilla extract

Preheat the oven to 175°C (fan oven 155°C), Gas Mark 4.

Mix the butter and sugar together until combined. Add the egg yolks and mix again. Add half of the flour and continue mixing slowly, then add the remaining flour, salt and cream and mix until you can no longer see any flour (about 30 seconds). Do not over-mix as this makes the dough tough.

Gently make a ball with the dough, then flatten into a disk. Cover in cling film and refrigerate for a minimum of 2 hours and up to 2 days.

Roll out the dough to about 7 mm (⅜ inch) thick and fit into a 20 cm (8 inch) deep pie dish. Shape the edge with your thumb and fingers. Prick the bottom with a fork and bake blind, using pie weights, for 20–30 minutes until the centre is just slightly golden. Remove from the oven and let cool.

For the filling, combine the egg yolks, whole eggs, sugar, lemon juice and zest in a bowl, mix well, then place over a pan of simmering water. Whisk over a medium heat until the mixture is very thick (about 5 minutes). Do not let it boil or the mixture will curdle.

Remove from the heat and mix in the butter, a quarter at a time, until well combined. Pour into the pie crust and let cool to room temperature.

For the topping, follow the recipe for American meringues (page 14). Spread the meringue over the lemon filling, covering very well right up to the edges of the crust. Make fancy peaks with the back of a spoon. Bake for 10–15 minutes until the peaks are golden and the meringue is no longer sticky to the touch. Cool to room temperature before serving.

Tip: Everyone always wants a second piece. But, if you need to store this pie, turn a large bowl upside-down to cover the pie and keep it in a cool, dry place. Placing cooked meringue in the refrigerator will cause the moisture to seep, resulting in little golden colour beads. This is not dangerous. Just not pretty.

Chocolate cupcakes with Italian meringue

Making Italian meringue is easier than it looks. And when it is finished it looks fabulous!

Preparation time: 15 minutes
Cooking time: 20–25 minutes
Makes 12 cupcakes

Chocolate cupcakes
75 g (2½ oz) cocoa powder
300 ml (10½ fl oz) boiling water
3 large eggs
1 teaspoon vanilla extract
280 g (10 oz) plain flour
300 g (10½ oz) caster sugar
1 tablespoon baking powder
¾ teaspoon salt
190 g (6¾ oz) butter, softened

Italian meringue
4 egg whites, at room temperature
200 g (7 oz) caster sugar
½ teaspoon vanilla extract

For the cupcakes, preheat the oven to 160°C (fan oven 140°C), Gas Mark 3.

Mix the cocoa powder and water together in a small bowl until smooth. Set aside.

Mix the eggs with a quarter of the cocoa mixture and the vanilla extract. In a large mixing bowl, combine the flour, sugar, baking powder and salt. Add the butter and the remaining cocoa mixture and beat slowly until all the dry ingredients are moist. Add the egg mixture in two batches, beating each for 30 seconds.

Spoon the mixture into cupcake moulds lined with paper cases. Fill the cases two-thirds full. The cupcakes will rise while baking and fall back a bit while cooling. Bake for 20–25 minutes until a skewer inserted into the cakes comes out clean.

Prepare the Italian meringue according to the recipe on page 14. Put all of the meringue into a piping bag with a small star nozzle. Starting in the centre of each cupcake, pipe little peaks all over. To achieve the height in the centre, pipe over the first layer of peaks. Allow to dry for a few minutes before using a cook's torch to caramelise the tips.

Chocolate swirl meringues

Adding more than the usual amount of chocolate to this classic makes them even better than usual.

Preparation time: 20 minutes
Cooking time: 1½ hours
Makes 6–8 large meringues

140 g (5 oz) dark chocolate
  (minimum 70% cocoa solids),
  broken into pieces
3 egg whites, at room temperature
150 g (5¼ oz) caster sugar

Preheat the oven to 90°C (fan oven 70°C), Gas Mark ¼. Line a baking sheet with baking parchment.

Melt the chocolate over a pan of simmering water or in the microwave and set aside.

Place the egg whites in a large metal bowl. Using an electric whisk, whisk on a medium speed for about 1 minute. The whites will turn to foam and begin to increase in volume. Increase the speed to high and continue until soft peaks begin to form. Still whisking, add the sugar a few spoonfuls at a time, whisking for 20–30 seconds after each addition. Continue to whisk until the egg whites are eight times their original volume, the sugar has dissolved and the mixture is stiff and shiny.

Gently pour the melted chocolate on to the meringue and, with one or two folding motions, fold the chocolate into the meringue. Do not mix well.

Spoon on to the baking sheet, making 6–8 cloud shapes about 10 cm (4 inches) round. Place in the oven for about 1½ hours or until the meringues are dry to the touch but have not changed colour. Allow to cool completely before removing from the baking parchment. The meringues will keep in an airtight container for up to 3 days.

Vacherin

This is an impressive looking and tasting dessert…and not that difficult to make.

Preparation time: 15 minutes
Cooking time: 30–40 minutes
Serves 6–8

900 g (2 lb) pistachio ice cream

Meringues
4 egg whites, at room temperature
200 g (7 oz) caster sugar

Preheat the oven to 90°C (fan oven 70°C), Gas Mark ¼. Line a baking sheet with baking parchment. Prepare a piping bag with a medium, round nozzle.

Make a double quantity of Classic meringues recipe (page 12). Fill the piping bag with a quarter of the meringue mixture.

Unless you have an enormous oven, you will have to make the meringue discs one or two at a time. Place an 18–20 cm (7–8 inch) metal ring in the centre of the baking sheet. Pipe the meringue inside the ring, working towards the middle (a little space between the spirals is okay). Remove the ring by pulling straight up and bake the meringue for 30–40 minutes until dry to the touch and still white.

Make the remaining three meringue discs and keep in a completely airtight container until you are ready to prepare the dessert.

Allow the ice cream to soften just enough so that you can spread it with a spatula. Working quickly, place one disc of meringue on a serving plate and cover with a third of the ice cream. Place the next disc on top and repeat twice more, finishing with the last meringue disc. Cut with a knife through all the layers to serve.

Mexican meringue chilli chips

When it's difficult to find real corn tortillas or to make real corn tortilla chips, what is a girl to do with a guacamole and chip craving? Make Mexican meringue chilli chips...what else! The light savoury but sweet flavour and crunch is perfect with guacamole or tomato salsa...or on their own...

Preparation time: 10 minutes
Cooking time: 15–20 minutes
Makes about 40 triangular chips

3 tablespoons dried instant polenta
2 egg whites, at room temperature
60 g (2 oz) caster sugar
¼ teaspoon salt
1 tablespoon dried coriander
¼ teaspoon chilli powder
¼ teaspoon ground black pepper
¼ red pepper, de-seeded and sliced
   into very thin 2–4 cm (¾–1½ inch)
   long strips

Preheat the oven to 90°C (fan oven 70°C), Gas Mark ¼. Line two baking sheets with baking parchment (see Tip). Sprinkle 1 tablespoon of polenta on to the baking parchment. Prepare a piping bag with a plain 5–6 mm (¼ inch) nozzle.

Follow the recipe for Classic meringues (page 12), whisking until soft peaks begin to form. Still whisking, add the sugar gradually, a few spoonfuls at a time, and whisk until the mixture is stiff and shiny. Slowly add the salt, coriander, chilli powder and black pepper and whisk for 20–30 seconds.

Put the mixture into the piping bag. For each chip, pipe out thin, 5 cm (2 inch) triangles. Space the meringues about 4 cm (1½ inches) apart. Using a knife or flat metal spatula, smooth the chips. Sprinkle a few red pepper strips on each chip, then sprinkle on a pinch of polenta.

Bake for about 15–20 minutes or until the chips are dry to the touch and just starting to go a little golden. Allow to cool completely before removing from the baking parchment. Store in an airtight container for up to 3 days.

Tip: If your oven or baking sheets are not large enough to bake all the chips, have two pieces of baking parchment ready. Pipe out the remaining meringue on to the second piece of paper, ready to go in the oven as soon as the first is done.

Moroccan meringue flatbread

These meringues, masquerading as oriental flatbreads, go wonderfully with yogurt and tahini.

Preparation time: 30 minutes
Cooking time: 20 minutes
Makes 2 large meringues

Moroccan meringues
2 egg whites, at room temperature
80 g (2¾ oz) caster sugar
½ teaspoon Ras-el-Hanout
⅛ teaspoon garlic powder
¼ teaspoon salt
6 fresh mint leaves, chopped
3 teaspoons pine nuts
2 teaspoons black sesame seeds

Yogurt tahini dip
4 tablespoons tahini
1 tablespoon salt
2–3 tablespoons lemon juice, to
  taste
125 g (4½ oz) plain, full fat yogurt
1 tablespoon black sesame seeds

Preheat the oven to 90°C (fan oven 70°C), Gas Mark ¼. Line a baking sheet with baking parchment.

Follow the recipe for Classic meringues (page 12), whisking the egg whites and gradually adding the sugar until the mixture is stiff and shiny. Slowly add the Ras-el-Hanout, garlic powder and salt and whisk for another 20–30 seconds.

With a large spatula, place half of the mixture on one side of the baking sheet, creating a 22 cm (8½ inch) long, 10–12 cm (4–4½ inch) wide shape. Do the same with the remaining mixture on the other side of the sheet. Sprinkle the chopped mint, pine nuts and sesame seeds over both flatbreads.

Bake for about 20 minutes or until the meringues are dry to the touch. Allow to cool for about 5 minutes before gently removing from the baking parchment with a spatula. The meringues can be stored in an airtight container for up to 5 days.

For the dip, mix together the tahini, salt, lemon juice and yogurt until they are well combined. Add the sesame seeds. Gently break the breads with your hands and serve with the dip.

Wasabi meringue canapés with crab and sesame

I have a problem with this recipe… No matter how many I make, it seems it is never enough.

Preparation time: 15 minutes
Cooking time: 20 minutes
Makes 24–30 canapés

Meringue canapés
1 teaspoon olive oil
2 shallots, thinly sliced into rounds
2 egg whites, at room temperature
60 g (2 oz) caster sugar
¼ tablespoon salt
¼ teaspoon wasabi powder
2 teaspoons sesame seeds

Crab and sesame topping
150 g (5¼ oz) crab meat, cooked
1–2 teaspoons lemon juice
1–2 teaspoons lime juice
a few pinches of salt
1 teaspoon wasabi powder
500 ml (17½ fl oz) crème fraîche
a few chives, snipped

Preheat the oven to 90°C (fan oven 70°C), Gas Mark ¼. Line a baking sheet with baking parchment.

Heat the oil in a non-stick pan over a medium heat and cook the shallots until golden and starting to caramelise. Remove from the pan and place on kitchen towel to absorb the excess oil. Set aside.

Follow the Classic meringues recipe (page 12), whisking the egg whites and gradually adding the sugar until the mixture is stiff and shiny. Add the salt and wasabi powder and whisk for a further 20–30 seconds.

Using a tablespoon, place a dollop of meringue on the baking sheet. With the back of the spoon, make a small crater in the centres. Repeat with the rest of the mixture, leaving 3–4 cm (1¼–1½ inches) between each meringue. With your fingers, sprinkle a pinch of shallots on each meringue, then a pinch of sesame seeds. Be messy, these should not look neat!

Bake for about 20 minutes until the meringues are dry to the touch. Allow to cool completely before removing from the baking parchment. The meringues can be stored in a very airtight container for up to 3 days.

Separate the crab meat with a fork, leaving pieces of various sizes. Add 1 teaspoon each of lemon and lime juice and a pinch of salt. Taste and add additional lemon and lime juice and salt if necessary.

Mix the wasabi powder and crème fraîche together well.

Keep the crab meat and wasabi cream in the refrigerator until you are ready to assemble the canapés.

To assemble, place a spoonful of the crab meat on to each meringue, drizzle over some of the wasabi cream then sprinkle with a few chopped chives. Serve immediately.

Crayfish meringue nests

I have a large music collection that inspires new recipes or reminds me of past occasions and what was eaten...(it's always about the food). The idea for this Cajun-esque meringue came to me after listening to one of my favourite American artists.

Preparation time: 15 minutes
Cooking time: 20–30 minutes
Serves 6

Meringue nests
2 egg whites, at room temperature
80 g (2¾ oz) caster sugar
½ teaspoon lemon salt or regular salt
¼ teaspoon ground black pepper

Crayfish filling
120 g (4¼ oz) mayonnaise
1 tablespoon ketchup
½ teaspoon mustard powder
½ teaspoon paprika
½ shallot, minced
a few drops of lemon juice
30 g (1 oz) butter
30 crayfish, raw, cleaned and removed from their shells
a few pinches of salt

Preheat the oven to 90°C (fan oven 70°C), Gas Mark ¼. Line a baking sheet with baking parchment. Prepare a piping bag with a 1 cm (½ inch) round nozzle.

Follow the Classic meringues recipe (page 12), whisking the egg whites and gradually adding the sugar until the mixture is stiff and shiny. Add the salt and pepper and whisk for a further 30 seconds.

Put the mixture into the piping bag. Make six nests on the baking sheet by piping a flat, 6 cm (2½ inch) base then building up the sides with three layers of straight piping.

Bake for about 20–30 minutes or until the meringues are dry to the touch and still white in colour. Allow the nests to cool for 10 minutes before gently removing from the baking parchment.

For the sauce, combine the mayonnaise, ketchup, mustard powder, paprika, shallot and lemon juice. Set aside in the refrigerator.

In a non-stick frying pan, melt the butter over a medium heat. Add the crayfish and cook for about 5 minutes, stirring occasionally. They are done when they turn rosy and the flesh is no longer translucent. Turn off the heat and add salt to taste.

Fill the meringues with the crayfish. Drizzle the sauce over the crayfish and nests just before serving.

Parmesan meringue sticks

These are so light. They are lovely accompanied by a good olive oil and salt.

Preparation time: 10 minutes
Cooking time: 25–30 minutes
Makes 8–10 sticks

2 egg whites, at room temperature
60 g (2 oz) caster sugar
½ teaspoon salt
½ teaspoon ground black pepper
120 g (4¼ oz) Parmesan cheese,
  thickly grated

Preheat the oven to 90°C (fan oven 70°C), Gas Mark ¼. Line two baking sheets with baking parchment (see Tip). Prepare a piping bag with a large round nozzle.

Place the egg whites in a large metal bowl. Using an electric whisk, whisk on a medium speed for about 1 minute. The whites will turn to foam and begin to increase in volume. Increase the speed to high and continue until soft peaks begin to form. Still whisking, add the sugar a few spoonfuls at a time, whisking for 20–30 seconds after each addition. Add the salt and pepper and continue to whisk until the egg whites are six times their original volume, the sugar has dissolved and the mixture is stiff and shiny.

Put the mixture into the piping bag. Pipe out 16 cm (6¼ inch) long sticks on the baking sheets, placing them 4 cm (1½ inches) apart.

Bake for 20 minutes. Leaving the oven on, remove the sheet, sprinkle Parmesan cheese on all of the meringue sticks and return to the oven for 5–10 minutes until the cheese is melted but not bubbling. Allow the meringues to cool for 5 minutes before gently removing from the baking parchment with a spatula.

Tip: If your oven or baking sheets are not large enough to bake all the sticks, have two pieces of baking parchment ready. Pipe out the remaining meringue on to the second piece of paper, ready to go in the oven as soon as the first is done.

Meringue fougasse with olives and rosemary

This meringue is 100% Provençale!

Preparation time: 10 minutes
Cooking time: 30–40 minutes
Makes one large or two medium
fougasse

Meringue fougasse
2 egg whites, at room temperature
60 g (2 oz) caster sugar
½ teaspoon salt
1 tablespoon dried rosemary
1 sprig fresh rosemary
12–15 black olives, stoned

To serve
olive oil
smoked sea salt

Preheat the oven to 90°C (fan oven 70°C), Gas Mark ¼. Line a baking sheet with baking parchment. Prepare a piping bag with a large round nozzle.

Place the egg whites in a large metal bowl. Using an electric whisk, whisk on a medium speed for about 1 minute. The whites will turn to foam and begin to increase in volume. Increase the speed to high and continue until soft peaks begin to form. Still whisking, add the sugar and salt gradually, whisking for 20–30 seconds after each addition. Continue to whisk until the egg whites are eight times their original volume, the sugar has dissolved and the mixture is stiff and shiny. Add the dried rosemary and whisk for a further 20 seconds.

Put the mixture into the piping bag. Pipe out one large (26 x 18 cm/ 10 x 7 inches) or two medium (18 x 14 cm/7 x 5½ inches) fougasse. Gently add the olives in a random-looking fashion and sprinkle over the fresh rosemary.

Bake for 30–40 minutes until the fougasse are slightly golden in colour and dry to the touch. Allow to cool for 5 minutes before gently removing from the baking parchment with a spatula. The meringues will keep in an airtight container for 2 days. Serve with olive oil for dipping and smoked sea salt.

Pepper meringue crackers

These crackers are really fast and easy. With one recipe, you will have four different pepper crackers. Serve with Basque cheeses such as Petit Basque or Ossau Iraty.

Preparation time: 10 minutes
Cooking time: 15–20 minutes
Makes 28–30 crackers

2 egg whites, at room temperature
80 g (2¾ oz) caster sugar
½ teaspoon salt
1 tablespoon ground black
  peppercorns
1 tablespoon ground red
  peppercorns
1 tablespoon ground green
  peppercorns
1 tablespoon paprika

Preheat the oven to 90°C (fan oven 70°C), Gas Mark ¼. Line two baking sheets with baking parchment (see Tip). Prepare a piping bag with a plain 5–6 mm (¼ inch) nozzle.

Place the egg whites in a large metal bowl. Using an electric whisk, whisk on a medium speed for about 1 minute. The whites will turn to foam and begin to increase in volume. Increase the speed to high and continue until soft peaks begin to form. Still whisking, gradually add the sugar and salt, whisking for 20–30 seconds after each addition. Continue to whisk until the egg whites are six times their original volume, the sugar has dissolved and the mixture is stiff and shiny.

Put the mixture into the piping bag. For each cracker, pipe out 4 cm (1½ inch) squares, 1 cm (½ inch) thick, spaced around 4 cm (1½ inches) apart. Using a knife or flat metal spatula, flatten the meringues, making them a bit larger but maintaining the square shape. Sprinkle seven or eight meringues with one of each type of pepper.

Bake for about 15–20 minutes or until the crackers are dry to the touch and just starting to turn golden. Allow to cool completely before gently removing them from the baking parchment. The meringues can be stored in a very airtight container for up to 7 days.

Tip: If your oven or baking sheets are not large enough to bake all the crackers, have two pieces of baking parchment ready. Pipe out the remaining meringue on to the second piece of paper, ready to go in the oven as soon as the first is done.

Meringue dippers with grilled onions and Gruyère cheese

OK…think outside the soup terrine here… Start with a classic, rich, onion soup recipe, but forget about the bread on the bottom or the cheese on top.

Preparation time: 40 minutes
Cooking time: 20–25 minutes
Makes about 10 dippers

1 teaspoon olive oil
2 onions, sliced into very thin
  rounds
2 egg whites, at room temperature
80 g (2¾ oz) caster sugar
1 teaspoon onion powder
¼ teaspoon dry garlic powder
¼ teaspoon salt
¼ teaspoon ground black pepper
250 g (8¾ oz) Gruyère cheese,
  grated

Put the olive oil in a medium-sized frying pan over a medium heat. Add the onions, stir to coat with oil and cook slowly for 10–20 minutes until the onions are caramelised and dark on the edges. Remove from the heat and set aside.

Preheat the oven to 90°C (fan oven 70°C), Gas Mark ¼. Line two baking sheets with baking parchment. Prepare a piping bag with a plain large nozzle.

Follow the Classic meringues recipe (page 12), whisking the egg whites and gradually adding the sugar until the mixture is stiff and shiny. Carefully add the onion powder, garlic powder, salt and pepper and whisk for 20–30 seconds.

Put the mixture into the piping bag. For each dipper, pipe out 14 cm (5½ inch) long meringues. Flatten with a knife or spatula to 4–5 cm (1½–2 inches) wide and 1 cm (½ inch) thick. Space the meringues about 4 cm (1½ inches) apart.

Bake for about 10–15 minutes. Leaving the oven on, remove the tray and place a few caramelised onions on each dipper. Sprinkle 1–2 teaspoons of grated cheese on top of each. Return to the oven for 5–10 minutes, until the cheese is melted but not bubbling. Allow the meringues to cool for 5 minutes before gently removing from the baking parchment with a spatula.

Serve with onion soup. You may never think of it the same way again.

Meringue and caviar millefeuille

Serve as an entrée, or a main course, with a salad or without… The sweet and salty flavours complement each other so well.

Preparation time: 10 minutes
Cooking time: 20–30 minutes
Serves 4

Meringues
2 egg whites, room temperature
a pinch of cream of tartar
55 g (2 oz) brown sugar
a pinch of salt
½ teaspoon vanilla extract

Caviar and cream filling
400 g (14 oz) crème fraîche
½ teaspoon lemon salt
2 teaspoons lemon zest
¼ teaspoon ground black pepper
100 g (3½ oz) caviar (or fish roe)

Preheat the oven to 150°C (fan oven 130°C), Gas Mark 2. Line a baking sheet with baking parchment.

In a medium bowl, mix the crème fraîche, salt, lemon zest and pepper. Set aside (it will keep for 2 days in the fridge).

Follow the recipe for Brown sugar meringues (page 16). Once the mixture sticks to an upturned spoon, it is ready to cook.

To form the meringue layers, use a spatula or pastry brush to paint the meringue on to the baking sheet, making sheets 1–2 cm (½–¾ inch) thick, 16–20 cm (6–8 inches) long and 6–7 cm (2½–2¾ inches) wide.

Bake for about 20–30 minutes or until the layers are dry to the touch. Allow the meringues to cool completely before removing from the baking parchment.

Break or cut each meringue in half (these look pretty if the layers are not all the same length). Assemble in layers with the cream and caviar just before serving.

Calamari with meringue onion rings

Preparation time: 15 minutes
Cooking time: 20–30 minutes
Serves 6–8 as a starter

Meringue onion rings
2 egg whites, at room temperature
80 g (2¾ oz) caster sugar
½ teaspoon salt
1 teaspoon ground black pepper
2 tablespoons dried onion flakes

Calamari
250 g (8¾ oz) frozen squid rings
250 g (8¾ oz) frozen squid
  tentacles
200 g (7 oz) plain flour
1 teaspoon salt
1 teaspoon ground black pepper
oil, for frying

Preheat the oven to 90°C (fan oven 70°C), Gas Mark ¼. Line two baking sheets with baking parchment. Prepare a piping bag with a large five-star nozzle.

Follow the recipe for Classic meringues (page 12), whisking the egg whites and gradually adding the sugar until the mixture is stiff and shiny. Add the salt, pepper and 1 tablespoon of the onion flakes and continue to whisk until the egg whites are six times their original volume and stiff and shiny.

Put the mixture into the piping bag. Pipe 7 cm (2¾ inch) rings on to the baking sheet, spacing the rings about 4 cm (1½ inches) apart. Sprinkle the remaining onion flakes over the rings and bake for 20–30 minutes or until they are dry to the touch and just starting to turn a little golden. Allow the meringues to cool for 5 minutes before gently removing from the baking parchment.

Frozen squid is perfect for this recipe. Since the frying time is a little different, prepare and fry the rings and the frilly tentacle parts separately. Thaw the squid and strain, removing as much water as possible. Transfer to kitchen towels and pat to remove more moisture. Don't make yourself crazy over this – they do not need to be completely dry.

In a large bowl, mix together the flour, salt and pepper. Place the rings in the flour and toss to completely cover the squid. Shake off the excess flour before frying for 2–4 minutes. Do the same with the tentacles. Mix the two together and serve alongside the meringue onion rings.

Garlic meringue minarets with beetroot borscht

With grandparents of Russian descent, this cold soup was a recurring treat in our family gatherings. I love the bright flavours that are usually highlighted with a light sour cream. Garlic meringue minarets float and bring a new dimension to an old classic.

Preparation time: 20 minutes + cooling
Cooking time: 1½ hours
Serves 4–6

Garlic meringue minarets

2 teaspoons olive oil
2–3 large garlic cloves, sliced
2 egg whites, at room temperature
80 g (2¾ oz) caster sugar
1 teaspoon salt
1 teaspoon white pepper
1 teaspoon garlic powder

Beetroot borscht

1 litre (1¾ pints) water
4 medium raw beetroot, sliced into 1 cm (½ inch) rounds
1 onion, chopped
50 ml (1¾ fl oz) lemon juice
2 teaspoons fleur de sel (or regular sea salt)
50 g (1¾ oz) caster sugar

Preheat the oven to 90°C (fan oven 70°C), Gas Mark ¼. Line a baking sheet with baking parchment. Prepare a piping bag with a 1.5 cm (½ inch) round nozzle.

Warm the oil in a small pan. Add the sliced garlic and cook until light golden in colour. Remove from the oil, drain on kitchen towel and set aside.

Follow the Classic meringues recipe (page 12), whisking the egg whites and gradually adding the sugar until the mixture is stiff and shiny. Add the salt, pepper and garlic powder. Continue to whisk until all the ingredients are mixed in. The meringue is ready for baking when it doesn't slide off a spoon and it holds its shape.

Put the mixture into the piping bag. Pipe out 3–4 cm (1¼–1½ inch) round, pointed meringues on to the baking sheet, about 3 cm (1¼ inches) apart from each other. Bake for about 20 minutes. Remove the sheet from the oven just long enough to place one slice of garlic on each minaret. Return to the oven for about 10 minutes or until they are dry to the touch and still white in colour. Allow to cool completely before removing from the baking paper. These can be stored in an airtight container for up to 3 days.

Boil the water in a large saucepan and add the beetroot. Add the onion, lemon juice, salt and sugar and boil for 1 hour. Let the soup cool, then remove the beetroot from the soup, cut into 5 mm (¼ inch) strips and return to the broth. Refrigerate until cold. Serve cold with floating garlic meringues on top.

Meringue sushi

An alternative to rice....

Preparation time: 35 minutes
Cooking time: 20 minutes
Makes 12 sushi

Meringues
2 egg whites, at room temperature
80 g (2¾ oz) caster sugar
½ teaspoon salt
¼ teaspoon celery salt
1–2 teaspoons wasabi sesame
  seeds

Sushi
250 g (8¾ oz) raw sushi grade tuna
2–3 sheets nori seaweed, cut into
  14 x 2 cm (5½ x ¾ inch) strips

To serve
soy sauce
pickled ginger
wasabi

Preheat the oven to 90°C (fan oven 70°C), Gas Mark ¼. Line a baking sheet with baking parchment. Prepare a piping bag with a 1 cm (½ inch) round nozzle.

Place the egg whites in a large metal bowl. Using an electric whisk, whisk on a medium speed for about 1 minute. The whites will turn to foam and begin to increase in volume. Increase the speed to high and continue until soft peaks begin to form. Still whisking, gradually add the sugar, salt and celery salt, whisking for 20–30 seconds after each addition. Continue to whisk until the egg whites are eight times their original volume, the sugar has dissolved and the mixture is stiff and shiny.

Put the mixture into the piping bag. Pipe back and forth to create shapes about 2 cm (¾ inch) wide and 6 cm (2½ inches) long. Pull the piping bag up at the end to create a little peak, spacing the meringues about 3 cm (1¼ inches) apart. Sprinkle over the wasabi sesame seeds and bake for about 20 minutes or until they are dry to the touch and just starting to turn golden. Allow the meringues to cool completely before removing from the baking parchment. They can be stored in an airtight container for up to 5 days.

Assemble just before serving. Have a small dish of water ready. Cut the tuna into 2 x 6 x 1.5 cm (¾ x 2½ x ½ inch) rectangles. Place a meringue on top of each piece of tuna and wrap with a strip of seaweed. To stick the seaweed together, dip your finger into the water and moisten the ends, pressing together gently. Serve with soy sauce, pickled ginger and wasabi.

Index

Conversion tables

The tables below are only approximate and are meant to be used as a guide only.

Approximate American/ European conversions

	USA	Metric	Imperial
brown sugar	1 cup	170 g	6 oz
butter	1 stick	115 g	4 oz
butter/ margarine/ lard	1 cup	225 g	8 oz
caster and granulated sugar	2 level tablespoons	30 g	1 oz
caster and granulated sugar	1 cup	225 g	8 oz
currants	1 cup	140 g	5 oz
flour	1 cup	140 g	5 oz
golden syrup	1 cup	350 g	12 oz
ground almonds	1 cup	115 g	4 oz
sultanas/ raisins	1 cup	200 g	7 oz

Approximate American/ European conversions

American	European
1 teaspoon	1 teaspoon/ 5 ml
½ fl oz	1 tablespoon/ ½ fl oz/ 15 ml
¼ cup	4 tablespoons/ 2 fl oz/ 50 ml
½ cup plus 2 tablespoons	¼ pint/ 5 fl oz/ 150 ml
1¼ cups	½ pint/ 10 fl oz/ 300 ml
1 pint/ 16 fl oz	1 pint/ 20 fl oz/ 600 ml
2½ pints (5 cups)	1.2 litres/ 2 pints
10 pints	4.5 litres/ 8 pints

Liquid measures

Imperial	ml	fl oz
1 teaspoon	5	
2 tablespoons	30	
4 tablespoons	60	
¼ pint/ 1 gill	150	5
⅓ pint	200	7
½ pint	300	10
¾ pint	425	15
1 pint	600	20
1¾ pints	1000 (1 litre)	35

Oven temperatures

American	Celsius	Fahrenheit	Gas Mark
Cool	130	250	½
Very slow	140	275	1
Slow	150	300	2
Moderate	160	320	3
Moderate	180	350	4
Moderately hot	190	375	5
Fairly hot	200	400	6
Hot	220	425	7
Very hot	230	450	8
Extremely hot	240	475	9

Other useful measurements

Measurement	Metric	Imperial
1 American cup	225 ml	8 fl oz
1 egg, size 3	50 ml	2 fl oz
1 egg white	30 ml	1 fl oz
1 rounded tablespoon flour	30 g	1 oz
1 rounded tablespoon cornflour	30 g	1 oz
1 rounded tablespoon caster sugar	30 g	1 oz
2 level teaspoons gelatine	10 g	¼ oz